Colonial Cooking

A Treasury of Colonial Recipes

By Rebecca Caruba

Hammond Incorporated
Maplewood, New Jersey

Library of Congress Cataloging in Publication Data
Caruba, Rebecca.
    Colonial Cooking: a treasury of colonial recipes.
    Includes index.
    1. Cookery, American.   2. United States — History —
Colonial period, ca. 1600 — 1775.   I. Title.
TX715.C32   641.5'973   75-13656
ISBN 0-8437-3226-1
ISBN 0-8437-3225-3 pbk.

Printed in the United States of America

Contents

INTRODUCTION

New Engand Clam Chowder, Indian Pudding, Roast Turkey, Shrimp Gumbo, Boston Baked Beans, Corn Bread, Sweet Potato and Cranberry Casserole, Pumpkin Pie — these traditional American dishes, reflecting the richness and variety of our culinary heritage, all have colonial origins. Colonial cooking was typically American, initially plain but hearty and satisfying and, with increasing affluence and the passing of time, often very elegant.

The abundance and variety of food which has characterized America was not immediately apparent to the first settlers, some of whom starved in early Jamestown. However, the colonists soon learned to cope with their new land, and before long their farms yielded ample produce to feed growing families.

With the help of the Indians the colonists began to grow and use the unfamiliar foods they found — corn, rice, the many varieties of beans, squash, pumpkins, sweet potatoes, cranberries and blueberries. From their European homelands the settlers introduced familiar leaf vegetables and carrots, turnips and other root crops, The orchards were planted with apple, peach and pear trees, and berries of all kinds were grown.

The woodlands were rich in wild turkey, geese, pheasant, ducks and game animals of many kinds. The streams yielded many varieties of freshwater fish, and the ocean provided oysters, clams, shrimp, crabs and lobsters in addition to cod, halibut, herring and whitefish. Cattle, sheep and pigs proliferated, providing beef, veal, pork, milk, butter and cheese.

The most famous farmer of them all was Thomas Jefferson, our third President. He grew peas, both early and late, lettuce, cucumbers, watermelons, Indian corn, and such exotic vegetables as broccoli, endive and tomatoes.

Having spent five years in Paris as the United States envoy, Jefferson had developed a great enthusiasm for French cuisine. He was first to bring a chef back from France to cook with the native foods and, in turn, teach his assistants his own methods of preparing French dishes from the abundance he found at Jefferson's Monticello estate.

Historians tell us that Jefferson also brought back the first vanilla beans from France. He had tasted the vanilla-flavored desserts there and wanted to introduce them to his friends at home. Entertainment was so lavish at Monticello that the 200 vanilla beans did not even last a year, and Jefferson wrote to one of his French friends asking him to be kind enough to send him more.

We credit New England sea captains, who plied their way to the West Indies and South American countries, with introducing cocoa beans into the colonies. These captains traded sugar and rum for them in exchange. The first American chocolate factory was established in 1765, and it was so successful that chocolate was to become the favorite flavor in this country, as it is to this day.

The wives of the colonists could also purchase salt, spices, cane sugar and molasses. Spices in colonial America were very costly and highly valued, as they were essential to preserving food and in disguising spoiled food. Some were even brewed as medicines. They were often sold in apothecary shops such as can be visited in the recreated colonial town in Williamsburg, Virginia.

There were no modern ovens, no year-round refrigerators, but there *were* smokehouses, and the colonists knew the art of preserving. Meats were smoked, salted and dried, or pickled in brine. Cold cellars were dug to hold root vegetables and apples over the winter. Fruits were used fresh or dried in pies, puddings and preserves.

In the earliest days cooking was limited to a few basic dishes but, as life in America became more than a fight for survival and the population became polyglot, cooking developed greatly in subtlety and variety. America in its first years attracted not only the English, but others, such as the Dutch, French, Rhineland Germans, Scotch-Irish, Scots and Spaniards. They brought with them treasured family recipes for breads, pies, puddings and stews, and they constantly sent back to their original homelands for spices to replenish their larders. Out of the need to adapt the old heritage to new requirements many new recipes were developed. Homemakers from these many lands exchanged cooking and baking ideas both old and new at quilting bees and after church.

When one realizes that cooking in colonial times was done in huge open fireplaces in the kitchen, one can understand why these kitchens were in the basement or, in the South, sometimes housed in a separate building so that the family did not have to inhale the odors of the cooking or suffer from the heat. Some kitchens even boasted two: one for the side of a large animal and a smaller one for the wild birds and fish that abounded. The kitchen ceilings were usually higher than in any other part of the house and, to make the floor fireproof, it was usually made of brick or left as earth with no covering. The walls of the kitchen were whitewashed frequently to cover the soot, and many layers were accumulated over the years.

The built-in fireplace had a chimney bar, one or sometimes two movable cranes and a brick oven for baking. The oven had its own wrought-iron door so that smoke from the open fire would not flavor whatever was baking in the oven, but would go up the chimney.

Many kinds of equipment had to be made for these huge fireplaces. The tongs and long-handled shovels used to remove the baked breads and pies from the oven had to be fashioned by hand. They also served to move hot coals or logs about the hearth when more heat was needed in a particular spot. Pot racks were fashioned with an arrangement to lower or raise the pots that hung on them. Chain hangers had loops to fit over the hooks to hold the pots in place. A clever person could also fashion a "hastener," which was a metal shield that stood by the fireplace. When a pot of stew was not cooking fast enough, or the spit holding the meat for roasting was too slow, the shield was placed at the opening of the fireplace, keeping the heat inside to "hasten" the cooking.

What we call andirons were called firedogs then, and these held the roasting spits, which were of different lengths and weights for different sizes of meat and fowl. Some of these spits had to be turned by hand and came equipped with a handle for the purpose. Another feature of the spit was an attachment to hold the roasting meat in place as it turned. These were forklike prongs much like those on spits used today. There were always a dripping pan made of iron to catch the juices and a long-handled basting spoon to keep the meat moist.

The kitchen furniture usually consisted of rows of shelves, some chests, a table and chairs which also served as an eating area for the servants. Some kitchens had cabinets that displayed the hand-wrought pewter and crockery. They served to store supplies and utensils for cooking and, most important, these cabinets could be locked to safeguard precious spices. A large table served as a working area to roll out pies and pastries.

Holidays called for traditional dishes and special effort to provide a dinner more ample and memorable than usual. Christmas at Mount Vernon was no exception. George and Martha Washington had been married on the twelfth night of Christmas in 1759 and, throughout their lives, arranged to spend the Christmas holiday together. Christmas dinner at Mount Vernon was served at three o'clock in the afternoon and consisted of three courses. The hour selected allowed for a long time to be spent enjoying each element of the meal.

It started with King's soup, which was followed by oysters on the half-shell, roast beef and Yorkshire pudding, mutton chops, roast suckling pig, roast turkey with chestnut stuffing, cold baked Virginia ham, lima beans, baked acorn squash, braised celery with almonds, hominy pudding, sweet potatoes, spiced peaches in brandy, spiced cranberries, mincemeat pie, apple pie, plum pudding, fruits, nuts and raisins.

A fine red wine from Bordeaux, France, which the English call Claret, was served with dinner.

History tells us that it was customary to toast each individual guest by name, and this custom was followed by the President. Each guest would toast each other in turn, and this went on and on throughout the meal. No wonder they were able to consume such great quantities of food. The wine served as a natural aid to good digestion.

Dinner at Mount Vernon was concluded with Port and Madeira, which were served with the tea. Madeira, a first cousin to Sherry, was brought to this country by the Pilgrims. It was their "medicine" to help them keep in good health!

Preparations for the Christmas feast began weeks in advance. The wild turkey must be hunted, the cow and the pig butchered, dressed and kept in the cold cellar. The relishes, the jams and the jellies had been preserved long before. The plum pudding was made and left to mellow in the cellar. When Christmas came, it was laced with brandy in the kitchen and brought to the table flaming, with the hard sauce to accompany it.

In this book of remembrance you will find many recipes from colonial days. From them memorable colonial meals can be created in a manner to fit our times, our appetites and our purses.

It would be impossible for the modern homemaker to use the recipes the colonists gave us in their original form. I offer you a selection of recipes streamlined to today's modern equipment and to modern tastes, and I urge you to take an imaginary journey back through time as you dine with the Pilgrims and pioneers of early America.

Rebecca Caruba
1975

SOUPS

Soups and stews served as the main meal for most colonists, so they had to be substantial. Soup containing meat and vegetables and served with bread from the oven was truly the staff of life in early America.

The colonists prepared many kinds of soups, gruels, broths, and porridges, all in the same large pot that hung in the fireplace. Rules were given as to the cleaning of the soup pot to get rid of the flavor of the previous day's soup or stew. Soup was distinguished from stew by the addition of more vegetables and more water. There were also clear broths prepared for invalids and, if all was not consumed, they served as a stock to be added to the stew to flavor it. Gruel was soup thickened with barley, oatmeal or farina with perhaps some milk, wine or ale added. It was then sweetened and seasoned with spices.

Many soups, like stews, contained meat, sometimes carrots, onions and turnips with a few greens, all washed and cleaned before going into the pot. Soups and stews were made from beef, fowl, veal, ham, and turtle. Just about anything that could be hunted, such as rabbit and raccoon, was combined with the ingredients in the pot and flavored with herbs and spices. The end result was a delicious dish.

King's Soup

2 tbsp butter
1 very large onion
1 quart milk
1 quart chicken stock

⅛ tsp salt
⅛ tsp grated nutmeg
1 egg yolk
Croutons

Peel the onion and cut in half with a very sharp knife. Slice each half paperthin. Melt the butter in a 3-quart pot and add the sliced onion. Cook 5 minutes, then add the milk, stock, salt and nutmeg. Cook over very low heat for 20 minutes to incorporate the flavors. Pour ¼ cup of the soup into a small bowl. Add the egg yolk and beat well or until the mixture thickens a bit. Pour into the soup and stir. Place 4-5 croutons (toasted slices of white bread cut into small squares) in the bottom of each bowl, pour in the soup and serve.

makes 6-8 servings

Pumpkin Soup

3 cups milk
2 cups pumpkin puree (freshly
   prepared or canned)
2 tbsp butter
1 tsp sugar
$\frac{1}{8}$ tsp salt
$\frac{1}{4}$ tsp ground white pepper
$\frac{1}{8}$ tsp ground mace or nutmeg
   Toasted bread slices

Pour the milk into a 2-quart pot and heat slowly until hot. Add the pumpkin puree, butter, sugar, salt and pepper. Add the spices and simmer very slowly for 3 or 4 minutes. Taste for seasoning and correct if necessary. Serve in bowls with a slice of white toast floating on top of each portion.

makes 4-6 servings

Black Bean Soup

2 cups dried black beans
2 quarts water
2 medium onions, chopped
3 ribs celery, chopped
4 whole cloves
1 tbsp Worcestershire
  sauce
⅛ tsp allspice

⅛ tsp thyme
1 piece bay leaf
  (size of dime)
1 tsp ground mustard seed
1 ham hock (1½-2 lb)
¼ cup sherry
2 hard-cooked eggs
1 fresh lemon

Soak the beans overnight in cold water to cover. Drain well and add 2 quarts of water, vegetables, seasonings and ham hock. Bring to a boil and cook over low heat for 2 hours or until the beans are tender. Remove ham and cut into small pieces. Put soup through the blender and return to the pot. Add the sherry and meat. Taste for seasoning. If too thick, add more water. Place a slice of egg atop a slice of lemon, float on the surface of each bowl and serve.

makes 6-8 servings — freezes well

Green Split Pea Soup

2 cups green split peas
3 ribs of celery
1 large onion, quartered
⅛ tsp salt
⅛ tsp pepper
1 tbsp beef glacé
   (concentrated beef base)
½ cup cooked ham

Place 3 quarts of water in a 5-quart pot. Rinse the split peas under running water and add to the pot. Add the celery cut in 4-inch lengths, the onion, salt and pepper. When the water is heated, add the beef glacé mixed with another cup of water to dissolve it. Bring to a boil and add ham. Simmer for an hour, then taste for seasonings and take from stove to cool. When cool, ladle the soup, including vegetables, 2 cups at a time into a blender. Blend until smooth, place in a clean pot and set aside to mellow. Heat before serving.

makes 3 quarts of soup — freezes well

Cream of Carrot Soup

2 tbsp butter
1 small onion, chopped
1 bunch fresh carrots,
  scraped & sliced
½ cup raw rice

1½ quarts chicken stock
2 cups milk
⅛ tsp salt
⅛ tsp white pepper
1 tsp sugar

Melt butter in a 3-quart pot. Add the onion and sliced carrots, cover and cook for 10 minutes. Add the rice and 1 quart of the chicken stock and cook for 30 minutes more or until rice is tender. Remove and put through a strainer. Pour back into the pot and add the remaining 2 cups of stock and the milk. Add an additional teaspoon of butter for flavor. Add the salt, pepper and sugar and taste, correcting seasoning if necessary.

makes 6 servings

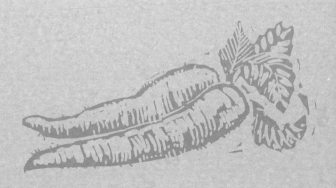

Potato and Onion Soup

2 tbsp butter
3 large potatoes, peeled
  & diced
2 large onions, chopped
1 tbsp flour
1 quart whole milk
1 cup water
½ tsp salt
⅛ tsp white pepper
Fresh or dried chives,
  chopped

Heat butter in a 3-quart pot and when melted add the potatoes and the onions. Cover and cook very slowly until both are soft. Sprinkle on the flour and toss until it disappears. Add the milk and water, then the salt and pepper and simmer until the milk takes on the other flavors (5 minutes). Remove from heat and put through the blender. Return to the pot, cover and let mellow until served. Add the chives as decoration.

makes 5-6 servings

Leek, Potato, Onion and Cabbage Soup

1 tbsp butter
4 leeks, sliced
3 medium potatoes, chopped
2 medium onions, chopped
2 cups shredded cabbage
6 sprays parsley, chopped
1 quart chicken stock
1 quart milk
⅛ tsp dill
⅛ tsp salt
⅛ tsp pepper
Croutons

Place the butter in a 5-quart pot and when melted add the washed and cleaned leeks and other vegetables. Cook slowly until they wilt (approximately 10 minutes). Add the hot stock, the milk and the seasonings, and cook 30 minutes until vegetables are tender and incorporated. Cool and put through the blender. Serve hot, garnished with croutons.

makes 8 servings

Cream of Watercress Soup

2 tbsp butter
3 leeks, sliced
1 medium onion,
  chopped
3 medium potatoes,
  sliced

3 cups chicken stock
1/8 tsp salt
1 cup milk
1/2 cup sherry
1 bunch fresh
  watercress

Melt butter in a 3-quart pot and slowly cook the leeks and onion in it. Add the potatoes, chicken stock and salt. Cook slowly for 25 minutes or until the potatoes are tender. Remove from fire and puree in the blender. Put back in pot, add milk and sherry and stir well.

Wash the watercress, dry on paper towels, discard the heavy stalks and place in a 1-quart pan with 1 cup of water. Cook over very high flame until it wilts. Drain and put through the blender. When liquified, add to the soup and mix well. May be served hot or cold.

makes 6-8 servings

Chicken Soup

1 3½-4 lb fowl	1 large carrot
4 quarts water	8 sprigs fresh parsley
1 large onion	⅛ tsp salt
2 ribs celery	

Place the cleaned chicken in a 5-quart pot and cover with the water. Bring to a boil, skim off the accumulated scum and discard. Add onion, celery, carrot, parsley and salt to the pot, cover and let cook for 1½ hours or until the fowl is tender. When tender and soup tastes hearty, remove the chicken to a dish and strain out the vegetables. Pour soup into a 2-quart pitcher and leave overnight to allow fat to rise to the top. Chicken may be removed from the bones and added to the soup or served separately. There should be 2 quarts of strong broth left. Garnish soup with parsley and serve with rice or fancy-shaped noodles.

makes 8 servings — freezes well

Corn and Chicken Chowder

1 large fowl	1 cup flour
3 quarts water	¼ cup milk
1 onion, sliced	1 whole egg
3 ribs celery,	2 cups corn kernels
chopped	2 hard-cooked eggs,
⅛ tsp salt	chopped

Clean chicken well and place in a 5-quart pot. Cover with approximately 3 quarts of water, the vegetables and salt. Cover and cook until chicken is tender or about 1 hour. Remove the chicken and let it cool; strip the meat from the bones, cut into small pieces and return to the pot. Make the dumplings by combining the cup of flour with the milk to make a crumbly mixture. Add the whole egg and combine into a paste. Drop small bits into the soup until all the flour mixture is used. Add the hard-cooked eggs and corn and cook the soup for 10 minutes until the dumplings are soft. Correct the seasoning if necessary and serve.

makes 6-8 servings

Beef and Wine Soup

2 tbsp butter
1 large onion, chopped
1 clove garlic, crushed
3 carrots, chopped
1½ cups celery, chopped
3 cups beef stock
2 cups white wine
2 cups tomato juice
2 cups diced leftover beef
⅛ tsp salt

Melt the butter in a 3-quart pot and sauté the onion in it till soft. Add the garlic, carrots and celery and cook until these are soft. Add the beef stock, wine, tomato juice and the beef. Simmer covered for 15 minutes to incorporate all the flavors. Season with salt and set aside until ready to serve. Serve with homemade noodles cut in squares.

makes 6-8 servings

Red Snapper Soup

First step:

1 3-lb red snapper, cut in pieces	6 sprigs parsley
1 quart water	3 whole cloves
1 small onion	1 tbsp butter
1 carrot	¼ cup diced onion
1 tsp thyme	½ cup diced celery
	½ cup diced pepper

Clean the snapper well. Remove head, tail and trimmings and place them in a skillet. Add the water, onion, carrot, thyme, parsley and cloves. Cover and simmer for 20 minutes to extract the flavor. Strain the fish stock, add pieces of fish and cook stock for 10 minutes. In another pot cook the diced onion, celery and pepper in the butter and add to the stockpot.

Second step:

3 tbsp butter	1 cup tomato puree
3 tbsp flour	1 tsp sugar
1 quart beef stock	2 tbsp brandy

Heat the 3 tablespoons of butter in a 3-quart pot and when melted add flour, beef stock, tomato puree and sugar. Add the fish stock and red snapper pieces and cook for 10 minutes. Add the brandy before serving.

makes 8 servings

New England Clam Chowder

1 quart clams with liquor
3 quarts water
2 4-inch by 2-inch slices
  salt pork, chopped
1 medium onion, sliced

3 medium potatoes,
  cubed
3 tbsp butter
2 cups cream or milk
1 tsp salt
$\frac{1}{8}$ tsp pepper

Combine clams, liquor and water in a 5-quart pot and bring to a boil. Drain, reserving the broth. Chop the clams and set aside. Fry the salt pork until lightly brown in color, then add the onion and cook 5 minutes. Add the clam broth and potato cubes and cook for 10 minutes or until the potato cubes are tender. Add the cream or milk, butter, salt and pepper. When ready to serve, heat the broth and pour into bowls. Serve with small biscuits.

makes 6-8 servings

Manhattan Clam Chowder

2 slices lean bacon
1 large onion, chopped
1 large potato, diced
1 pkg frozen mixed
  vegetables
1 16-oz can tomatoes
3 cups beef stock

⅛ tsp celery seed
⅛ tsp thyme
⅛ tsp caraway seed
⅛ tsp salt
⅛ tsp pepper
1 dozen chowder clams,
  minced

Cut the bacon in tiny pieces and place in a heated 3-quart pot to brown. Add onion, then the potato and cook 5 minutes until they are colored and tender. Add the mixed vegetables, tomatoes, stock and seasonings and simmer until vegetables are tender (approximately 7 minutes). Add the clams and cook *1* minute. Turn off heat until ready to serve.

makes 6 servings

Note: Although it is not known when Manhattan Clam Chowder was originated, it has been included for those who prefer it.

Cream of Clam Soup

4 tbsp butter	1/8 tsp chives
1 large onion, diced	2 tbsp flour
1 large potato, diced	1/4 cup dry white wine
1 rib celery, diced	2 cups milk
1/8 tsp salt	1 dozen cherrystone clams
1/8 tsp pepper	1 hard-cooked egg

Heat the butter in a 3-quart pot and when melted sauté the onion until golden. Add diced potato and celery and cook until both are tender. Add seasonings, then sprinkle on the flour, stirring until it is incorporated. Add the wine and milk and simmer a minute. Add the clams and continue to simmer for a few minutes to allow the soup to take on flavor. Press hard-cooked egg through a coarse strainer. Garnish soup with egg and serve.

makes 6 servings

Lobster and Celery Soup

3 tbsp butter	½ cup light cream
1 cup thinly sliced celery	¼ tsp thyme
2 tbsp chopped onion	⅛ tsp salt
3 tbsp flour	⅛ tsp pepper
3 cups milk	1 cup fresh lobster pieces
2 cups chicken stock	Parsley

Melt the butter in a 3-quart pot; add the celery and onion and cook till they wilt (5 minutes). Add the flour and stir quickly to incorporate. Add the milk, cream, stock and seasonings, stirring until thick. Add the lobster pieces and simmer for 3 minutes. Set aside until ready to serve. Sprinkle each bowl with chopped fresh parsley for color and flavor.

makes 6 servings

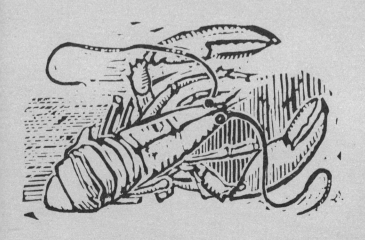

Lobster Chowder

4 tbsp butter	1 clove garlic, crushed
1 lb lobster meat (raw)	1 tsp Worcestershire sauce
2 tbsp flour	⅛ tsp salt
1 quart milk	⅛ tsp white pepper
1 cup light cream	⅛ tsp caraway
1 small onion, chopped	⅛ tsp thyme

In a 3-quart pot place 2 tablespoons of the butter and when melted add the lobster meat. Toss for 3-4 minutes or until it "blushes." Remove meat and set aside. Add the rest of the butter to the pot and when melted remove from the fire and add the flour. Mix well, then pour in the milk and cream, the onion and seasonings. Heat slowly, then add the lobster meat. Mix well, cover and set aside until ready to serve.

makes 6-8 servings

Cream of Crab Soup

3 strips lean bacon, diced
2 scallions or 1 small
    onion
1 cup crab meat, shredded
⅛ tsp salt
¼ cup sherry
4 cups chicken stock
¼ cup heavy cream
1 tbsp potato starch

Place the cut-up bacon pieces in a 3-quart pot and cook until crisp. Pour off the fat and add cut scallion or onion and cook 2 minutes. Add the crab meat, salt, sherry and chicken stock and bring to a boil. Combine the cream with the potato starch and add to the soup. This will thicken it. Cook a minute more and serve.

makes 6 servings

Note: If no potato starch is available, use corn-starch.

VICTUALS

The clambake and barbecue are time-honored methods of cooking which go back to the earliest colonial days. Before their homes were built, the hardy settlers learned to cook their food in the same manner as the Indians. They dug holes in the ground and lined them with hot stones, placing in the meat and covering the entire thing in order to preserve the heat. In another method of cooking which dates back to those same times, the colonists built a rack above an open fire; the meat was placed on the rack and periodically rotated by hand until they felt it was sufficiently cooked.

The racks were often large enough to hold up to six birds at a time.

After their homes were built, cooking moved indoors to the huge kitchen fireplaces. Meat and poultry were roasted over the fire on spits which were turned by hand. Meats and other foods were baked in the oven built into the side of the fireplace, where they cooked long and slowly. The most common method of cooking was in the stew pot, which hung over the fire. By adjusting the distance of the pot from the heat, the speed of cooking could be controlled so that it would be slow and even.

The chickens were not the pullets we find in the markets today, but the old, tired hens who had given many eggs. When they stopped laying they were considered ready for the stew kettle. Geese served several purposes, as their feathers were used to fill pillows and their quills were pens when sharpened and smoothed. Turkeys were also prized, not only for their feathers, but because they were very large. They could be stewed for an entire day to make them tender. Either leftover or fresh vegetables added flavor and nourishment to a soup which could be made from the carcass the next day. As animals, like chickens, were generally not slaughtered until they had outlived their usefulness for dairy or breeding, their meat was also usually cooked long and slowly to tenderize it.

Baked Steak

1 3-lb hip or sirloin steak
1 clove garlic, crushed
⅛ tsp salt
⅛ tsp pepper
⅛ tsp dry mustard
½ cup tomato sauce
1 onion, thinly sliced
⅛ tsp cayenne pepper
½ cup red wine

Prepare the steak by rubbing on the garlic, salt, pepper and dry mustard. Set aside until you prepare the roasting pan. Place the tomato sauce, onion, cayenne pepper and wine in the roasting pan. To be sure it does not overcook, put a meat thermometer in the steak. Heat oven to 350°. Place the steak in the pan, put in the oven and bake for 30 minutes or until it reaches the required doneness. Serve sliced on a heated platter and pour over it the gravy from the pan.

makes 4-6 servings

Beef and Pepper Fry

4 tbsp olive oil
2 green peppers
¼ lb fresh mushrooms, sliced
3 fresh tomatoes
⅛ tsp salt
⅛ tsp pepper
⅛ tsp sugar
⅛ tsp oregano
1 1-lb sirloin steak
¼ cup red wine

Place 2 tablespoons of oil in a 10-inch skillet to heat. Cut peppers in eighths, remove seeds and sauté in the oil until almost tender. Add the mushrooms, toss a minute, then add tomatoes skinned and cut into eighths. Add seasonings and remove the pan from the fire. Heat the other two tablespoons of oil in a smaller skillet and when very hot, add the steak cut into strips. Toss quickly for 2 minutes or until the meat loses its red color. Add the steak to the pan of vegetables, add the wine and quickly toss all together. Serve with mashed white potatoes or cooked wide noodles.

makes 4 servings

Beef and Beer Stew

2 lbs boneless chuck
1 tbsp butter
3 medium onions, sliced
1 large clove garlic
6 carrots, cut in 1-inch lengths
¼ tsp thyme
¼ tsp marjoram
⅛ tsp cayenne pepper
⅛ tsp salt
1 8-oz can beer
1 cup beef stock
2 cups raw potato balls

Cut meat into large squares. Heat butter in a 10-inch skillet; add meat and toss to sear in juices quickly. Remove the meat pieces from the pan and set aside. To the pan add onions, garlic, carrots and seasonings. Slowly add beer and stock and return the meat to pan. Cover and cook over low heat for an hour or until tender. Fifteen minutes before serving, add the potato balls, cover and cook until they are done. Be sure they do not fall apart!

makes 4-6 servings

Hearty Beef Stew

2 lbs beef
(chuck or crossrib)
1 tbsp flour
1 tbsp butter
1 large onion, sliced
1 clove garlic
1 rib celery, chopped

3 mushrooms, sliced
⅛ tsp salt
⅛ tsp pepper
1 small piece bay leaf
½ cup beef stock
2 tbsp tomato paste

Cut meat in 1-inch pieces, roll in the flour and pat dry. Sear the pieces in the butter in a large skillet and when browned all over remove them from the pan and set aside to establish a gravy. To the pan add the onion, garlic, vegetables, seasonings and stock. Add the tomato paste last and mix well to incorporate. Replace meat in pan, cover and cook until tender. Serve with mashed white potatoes.

makes 4-6 servings

Braised Leg of Mutton

1 7-lb mutton
  or lamb, boned
1 lb potatoes
2 tbsp butter
1 lb white navy beans
1 lb onions

2 cups beef stock
1/8 tsp rosemary
1/8 tsp basil
1/8 tsp salt
1/8 tsp pepper

Soak the beans overnight to soften them. Drain, add 2 cups fresh water and cook slowly for approximately 40 minutes until tender. Set these aside. Peel onions and slice them thin and sauté them in the butter until soft—not brown. Slice potatoes thin. Spread half of the onions on the bottom of a deep, 5-quart casserole, then spread half of the beans over the onions, half of the potatoes over the beans and continue until all the vegetables are used. Cut the boned mutton or lamb in half and lay the halves on top of the vegetables. Add the stock and seasonings and roast in a preheated 475° oven for 30 minutes, then reduce the heat to 350° and continue to cook until the lamb is done to your liking. Use a meat thermometer to be sure. Remove from oven, bring directly to the table and serve, cutting the meat in pieces, not slices.

makes 8-10 servings

Note: This was cooked in a large iron pot over the coals and checked very often.

Pork Chops and Apples

6 loin pork chops
2 tbsp flour
⅛ tsp salt
⅛ tsp pepper
6 apple rings
2 tbsp rum
1 tbsp red currant jelly (or apple)
1 tbsp fresh parsley, chopped

Wash and dry the chops with paper towels. Place the flour on a square of waxed paper. Dip each chop in the flour and dry it by patting well so there is just a dusting of flour on each chop. Heat a 10-inch skillet and when hot place the chops in it. Sauté until brown on one side (approximately 5 minutes), then turn and brown on the other side. The fat in the chops will run and be enough to brown them. Remove the chops to a baking dish. Peel and core the apple and slice into 6 rounds. Place a slice on each of the chops and in the center of each apple place a drop of jelly. Sprinkle with salt and pepper, pour the rum over the chops and bake in a preheated 375° oven for 30-35 minutes or until the chops are tender. Apple slice will be cooked through. Garnish with parsley and serve with cooked red cabbage.

makes 6 servings

Braised Pork Roast with Port Wine

1 loin of pork (5-6 lbs)
1 small onion, minced
½ cup tomato sauce
½ cup mushrooms, sliced
½ cup ruby Port wine

⅛ tsp sage
⅛ tsp salt
⅛ tsp pepper
⅛ tsp paprika

Trim as much fat as possible from the roast. Heat a deep, 5-quart pot and place the roast in it. The remaining fat on the loin will be enough to braise it. Turn to brown on both sides. Remove the roast until the gravy is established. Slice and add the mushrooms, the onion, tomato sauce, ¼ cup of the wine, then the seasonings to the pot. Stir until they are incorporated. Place the roast back in the pot, cover and cook for 50-60 minutes or until tender. Pork must be served well-done at all times. Pour in the other ¼ cup of Port wine just before removing from the pot, unless needed sooner to keep the sauce from becoming dry.

makes 6-8 servings

Chicken and Oysters

1 5-lb fowl	2 ribs celery
1 onion	4 sprigs parsley
1 carrot	⅛ tsp salt
3 dozen oysters	

Clean the chicken and place in a 6-quart pot. Add the vegetables, salt and water to cover and cook for 1½ hours or until chicken is tender. Remove the bird, cool, then remove all the meat and cut in bite-size pieces. Poach the oysters in their own juices for 3 minutes or just until the edges curl. Drain them from the juice and set aside, but reserve the juice.

Sauce:
3 tbsp butter
3 tbsp flour
Reserved oyster juice
½ cup heavy cream
½ cup white wine

Melt butter, blend in flour and the juice of the oysters. Add heavy cream and white wine. Stir the sauce over low heat until it thickens and pour it over the oysters and chicken pieces. Serve in a casserole over rice. This dish may be kept hot in the oven, but be careful that the oysters do not toughen.

makes 10-12 servings

Chicken-in-the-Pot

1 3-lb chicken
1 tbsp butter
12 small white onions
6 pieces carrot (½ cup)
6 pieces yellow turnip
  (½ cup)
6 pieces celery (½ cup)
4 pieces leeks (1 stalk)

5-6 mushrooms, quartered
1 tbsp tomato paste
1 cup white wine
2 tbsp sherry wine
1 cup chicken stock
⅛ tsp salt
⅛ tsp pepper
Freshly chopped parsley

Wash and dry the chicken. Cut into 8 pieces and brown skin-side-down in the heated butter in a large skillet. Add onions, carrot, turnip, celery and leek pieces and toss a minute. Add the mushrooms and tomato paste. Add the white wine and sherry and then the chicken stock. Cover and cook till tender (approximately 40 minutes). Put pieces of chicken in deep casserole and pour over it the vegetables. Sprinkle with the parsley and serve.

makes 4 servings

Potato Dumplings

2 large potatoes
½ cup milk
¼ cup butter
1 cup flour

2 whole eggs
⅛ tsp salt
½ tsp paprika
3 tbsp cheese

Boil peeled and cut potatoes until tender, strain and dry. Heat the milk to the boiling point and add the butter and flour quickly. Stir over the fire until the flour mixture forms a ball. Remove from heat and add the eggs, salt, paprika and cheese, then the dry potatoes. Mix well to incorporate and turn out on a floured working area. Roll into long strips and cut into 1-inch pieces. Have ready a 5-quart pot filled to ¾ with water, and when this is boiling drop in the dumplings and cook approximately 10 minutes. Drain in a collander and place on a large platter. Put in a 400° oven for 3 minutes to dry. Place on a serving dish and pour over it butter and additional cheese. Serve with meat or fowl.

makes 6-8 servings

Marrow Dumplings

¾ cup beef marrow	1 tsp parsley
1 cup soft, fresh bread crumbs	Nutmeg
	Salt
4 whole eggs	Pepper

Grind beef marrow and mix well with bread crumbs, eggs and parsley. Season with salt, nutmeg and white pepper to taste and let stand in refrigerator for 1 hour. Then shape the mixture into small balls the size of walnuts and poach them in simmering broth or gravy for 5 minutes. Serve with meat or fowl.

Farmer's Duckling

1 4-lb duckling
2 tbsp flour
1 medium can tomatoes or
   3 fresh tomatoes, chopped
2 leeks, chopped
½ cup white wine

2 carrots, chopped
2 ribs celery, chopped
3 sprigs parsley
½ clove garlic, crushed
⅛ tsp marjoram

Cut duckling in four serving pieces after washing and drying well. With a pair of kitchen shears remove as much fat as possible. Heat a 10-inch skillet and place the pieces of duckling skin-side-down in the pan. Render as much fat out of it as possible, draining the fat with a baster. When skin is brown and crisp, sprinkle the flour over the pieces. Add the tomatoes and other vegetables, seasonings and the wine. Cover and cook over low heat for 45 minutes or until duckling is tender. Mashed white potatoes go well with this dish.

makes 4 servings

Pheasant with Celery

1 pheasant	⅛ tsp salt
1 tbsp butter	⅛ tsp pepper
1 medium onion, chopped	1 cup white wine
1 carrot, chopped	1 bunch celery cut in 1-inch pieces

Pull off skin and clean pheasant inside and out. Cut into four serving pieces. Melt butter in 10-inch skillet and lay the pieces in. Add the onion, carrot, seasonings and wine but not the celery. Cover and cook until almost tender (approximately 45 minutes). Have celery cleaned and cut and add during the last 10 minutes of cooking. Place all the vegetables in a deep platter, lay the pieces of pheasant on top and serve.

makes 4 servings

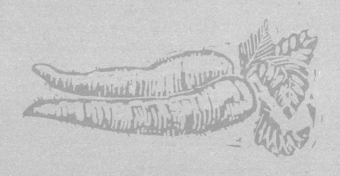

Roast Turkey

1 12-lb turkey
Powdered ginger
Rendered turkey, goose or
chicken fat
1 cup sherry

Clean the turkey inside and out. Remove the giblets and sprinkle the inside with powdered ginger. Dry well and set aside to receive the stuffing.

When stuffed, wipe the entire turkey with some rendered turkey, goose or chicken fat. Place turkey breast-side-down in an open roasting pan. Do not cover. Cut off enough cheesecloth to have three thicknesses of it to lay on the back of the bird. Grease this well with more fat or butter and set the turkey in a preheated (10 minutes) 350° oven.

After the turkey has cooked for an hour, start basting the bird with the cup of sherry every half hour. After 2½ hours, turn the turkey breast-side-up and continue to baste the breast until all the sherry is used and the bird is brown, shiny and beautiful. Allow 4½ hours for a 12-pound turkey.

makes 10 servings

Note: This is the way George Washington's Christmas turkey was prepared.

Chestnut Stuffing

2 tbsp fat from poultry, or same amount of butter

2 large onions, chopped fine

1 cup celery, chopped

1 cup parsley, chopped

3 slices day-old bread (white or assorted)

1 1-lb can of imported cooked & peeled chestnuts

¼ cup Madeira or sherry

⅛ tsp sage

⅛ tsp thyme

Put the fat in a 3-quart pot and when hot add the onions and celery. Sauté until they are soft (approximately 5 minutes). Take pot away from fire and add the parsley. Take two slices of bread at a time, run them under tap water. Squeeze out the water and add to the pot. Do this with the rest of the bread. Add the drained chestnuts and the Madeira or sherry, sage and thyme and toss all together. Place inside the turkey and sew the cavity with heavy string or seal with modern skewers.

Note: Never place the stuffing inside the turkey until just before roasting. Combustion may occur because of the chemicals added to the bread to keep it soft. Also the moist condition of the enclosed stuffing may cause harmful bacteria to form, resulting in food poisoning.

Deviled Haddock

¼ lb fresh mushrooms,
sliced
1 tbsp butter
1 cup white sauce
2 cups fresh haddock
2 tsp dry mustard

2 tbsp chopped parsley
1 tbsp Worcestershire
sauce
⅛ tsp marjoram
⅛ tsp salt
⅛ tsp pepper
3 slices white bread

Preheat oven to 350°. Sauté the mushrooms in the butter for a minute and combine with the white sauce. Break or cut the fish into small pieces and add to the sauce. Add mustard, parsley, Worcestershire sauce, marjoram, salt and pepper. Fold in ingredients gently and pour into a greased 1-quart casserole. Cover the top with bread crumbled in pieces. Bake uncovered for 30 minutes or until brown and bubbly on top.

White Sauce:
2 tbsp butter
2 tbsp flour
⅛ tsp salt

⅛ tsp pepper
⅛ tsp onion powder
⅛ tsp celery seed
1 cup milk

Melt butter in a 1-quart pan, remove from fire and add flour, salt, pepper, onion powder, celery seed and milk. Place pan back on fire and let come to a boil. Let rest until ready to use. Makes 1 cup of sauce.

makes 4 servings

Fish in Beer Sauce

1 can beer (your choice) 4 heavy fillets of sole
1 carrot, sliced   8 whole peppercorns
1 onion, sliced   5 whole cloves
1 rib celery   1 piece bay leaf size of dime

Pour the beer into a 10-inch skillet. Add the carrot, onion, celery and seasonings and let come to a boil. *Simmer* the vegetables for 10 minutes so that the beer takes on their flavors. Arrange the cleaned fish in the stock, cover and *simmer* for about 10 minutes or according to the thickness of the fish. When the fillets turn white, transfer them to a baking dish and let rest until the sauce is prepared.

Sauce: ¼ cup cream or milk
2 tbsp butter   ¼ cup grated Parmesan
2 tbsp flour   or Cheddar cheese
  Salt & pepper to taste ½ cup Swiss cheese
2 egg yolks   Parsley

Turn the heat under the skillet very high and cook until the juices reduce to 1 cup; strain. In a 1-quart pan melt the butter, remove from fire and add the flour, salt and pepper to taste. Put back on the fire, add the egg yolks and the cream or milk, stirring until smooth. Add the cheeses and stir until they are melted and the sauce is smooth. Pour this sauce over the fish and place under the broiler until top is golden and fish is very hot. Sprinkle with fresh chopped parsley and serve.

makes 4 servings

Poached Fish with Wine

3 cups water
1 cup white wine
1 rib celery
1 small onion
⅛ tsp white pepper
⅛ tsp salt

⅛ tsp caraway seeds
2 sprigs parsley
3 whole cloves
⅛ tsp thyme
2 large fish, cleaned
& skinned

Place the liquids in a 10-inch skillet. Add vegetables and seasonings and simmer for 10 minutes or until water takes on flavor. Add fish and cook for 8-9 minutes or until just firm. Remove fish carefully to large platter and reduce the liquid in the pan to 1 cup by turning the heat very high.

Sauce:
2 tbsp butter
2 tbsp flour
1 cup fish stock
½ cup cream
3 tbsp cheese
(your taste)

Melt butter in small pan and add flour, the fish stock and cream. Add the cheese and cook till smooth and thick. Pour sauce over fish, garnish with hard-cooked egg pressed through a coarse strainer and serve.

makes 4-6 servings

Party Crab Meat

3 tbsp butter	1/8 tsp marjoram
3 tbsp flour	1 cup milk
1/8 tsp salt	1 lb fresh or frozen
1/8 tsp white pepper	crab meat
1 tsp onion powder	1/4 cup sherry
	2 tbsp fresh parsley

Place the butter in the top of a 2-quart pot and when it is melted take away from the flame and add the flour, salt, pepper, onion powder, marjoram and milk. Mix well to remove lumps and place the pan directly over the heat to cook. Stir until the sauce is smooth and thickened, then add the crab meat and the sherry. Stir until all is heated. Sprinkle on the parsley and serve on toast points or cooked rice.

makes 8-10 servings

Scallops au Gratin

1 lb sea scallops
5 tbsp butter
4 tbsp flour
1½ cups milk
⅛ tsp salt
⅛ tsp white pepper
¼ lb Cheddar cheese, grated

Wash and dry scallops. Sprinkle on some lemon juice to freshen them. Place 1 tablespoon of butter in a 10-inch skillet and sauté the scallops for just 2 minutes. Prepare the sauce by melting 4 tablespoons of butter, adding the flour, then the milk and lastly the seasonings and cheese. Stir until sauce is smooth and add the scallops. Pour this mixture into a greased 1-quart casserole and when ready to serve place under the broiler until top is brown or place in a 450° oven for 10 minutes.

makes 4-6 servings

Shrimp Gumbo

2 tbsp oil	½ cup white wine
1 lb shrimp	⅛ tsp salt
2 medium onions, chopped	⅛ tsp pepper
1 sweet red pepper, chopped	4 fresh tomatoes
1 clove garlic, crushed	1 can okra or 1 lb fresh
1 tbsp flour	1 cup cooked rice
2 cups chicken stock	1 tsp gumbo filé

Place oil in 3-quart pot. Clean and devein shrimps. When oil is hot add shrimps and toss for 1 minute or until they turn pink. Remove them from pot and add onions, red pepper and garlic. Cook until soft, sprinkle on the flour and toss. Add stock, wine, salt, pepper, tomatoes and okra, and finally add the rice. Make a paste of the filé and 1 tablespoon of water and add. Add the shrimps, turn off heat and when ready to serve pour into a soup tureen.

makes 4 servings

Note: *gumbo filé is the dried bark of the sassafras tree and is easy to find in almost any store.*

Saddle of Venison with Bourbon

1 5-lb saddle of venison
½ cup bourbon whiskey
1 onion, sliced thin
1 carrot, sliced thin
6 whole peppercorns

6 whole cloves
⅛ tsp salt
⅛ tsp pepper
1 8-oz jar red currant
jelly

Wash and wipe the venison dry. Place in a very large bowl and pour over it the bourbon, vegetables and seasonings but not the jelly. Leave in the marinade for at least 2 hours, turning every half hour.

When ready to cook, remove meat and place it in a roasting pan. Make the sauce by melting the jelly in a 1-quart pan over low heat, adding the marinade and cooking a minute or two until it is smooth. Roast the venison for approximately 2½ hours, basting every half hour with the sauce until the meat is tender and shiny. If any sauce remains, serve it in a sauceboat.

makes 8-10 servings

Frog Legs Sauté

    3 or 4 frog legs per person
    Lemon juice
    1 whole egg
    2 tbsp water
    Flour to dry
    2 cloves garlic, crushed
    4 tbsp butter
    Watercress

Wash the frog legs well and dry. Sprinkle with the lemon juice. Beat the egg with the water. When ready to serve, dry the legs, dip first in the egg mixture then in flour and sauté in the garlic-butter mixture for 2 minutes on one side, then 2 minutes on the other. (To prepare garlic butter: Crush the garlic over the butter on a wooden board. With a wide, heavy spatula work them both together until very well blended.) Serve legs with tartar sauce or wedges of lemon on platter with watercress.

VEGETABLES

Few, if any, of the vegetable seeds that the first colonists brought with them took hold in the new land. However, the Indians showed them how to plant corn, raise sweet potatoes, squash, pumpkins and all kinds of beans. From these vegetables the colonists developed through experimentation many delicious dishes, ranging from soups to desserts.

They learned how to dry corn and beans and how to store them in cold cellars. Carrots, parsnips and other root vegetables were especially popular because of their keeping quality. These vegetables were used over the winter and in the months before the new crops were harvested.

Beans and corn appear to have been the staple vegetables upon which the colonists depended, and many different ways and combinations were devised to use them. Every woman prepared her

beans in the style of her community. In this way Vermont baked beans tasted different from Boston baked beans.

Tomatoes were not well known in colonial times and were considered poisonous by some. However, by the end of the colonial period they were commonly grown in some areas and were sold in the markets. We have included tomatoes in some recipes, since cooks must have been experimenting with them in keeping with the adventurous spirit of the times.

Although vegetables were often combined with meat, the colonists also devised tasty dishes in which vegetables were served singly or were used in combination with other vegetables or fruits.

Asparagus and Mushroom Casserole

1 lb cooked fresh
   asparagus, or 1 pkg
   frozen, cut asparagus
½ lb fresh mushrooms, sliced
2 tbsp butter
2 hard-cooked eggs

Cook the asparagus slowly in 1 tablespoon of butter in a covered pan until tender. Sauté the sliced mushrooms in the other tablespoon of butter for 5 minutes. Press the hard-cooked eggs through a coarse strainer and set all aside until sauce is prepared.

Sauce:

2 tbsp butter	⅛ tsp salt
2 tbsp flour	⅛ tsp pepper
1 cup milk	⅛ tsp celery seed
⅛ tsp onion powder	⅛ tsp paprika

Melt the butter in a 1-quart pot, remove pan from heat and add the flour, milk and seasonings except the paprika. Stir this away from heat until smooth, then return to the fire and cook slowly until it reaches the boil. Remove pan and set aside to prepare casserole.

To assemble: Place the asparagus in the bottom of a greased 1-quart casserole. Pour over it the mushrooms, then the eggs and, on top of all, the sauce. Sprinkle with paprika. Bake in a preheated 400° oven for 10-15 minutes or until heated through.

makes 6 servings

Glazed Carrots

1 bunch fresh, slender
   carrots
2 tbsp butter
2 tbsp dark brown
   sugar
⅛ tsp salt

Wash and brush the carrots. Melt the butter and sugar in an 8-inch skillet. Add the salt and then the carrots. Cover and let *simmer* on low heat until tender (approximately 7 minutes). Turn the carrots once to distribute the glaze.

makes 4 servings

Red Cabbage with Wine

2 tbsp butter
1 small onion, minced
1 2-lb head red cabbage
1 green apple, peeled & grated
½ cup red currant jelly
⅛ tsp salt
½ cup red wine
1 tbsp flour

Place the butter in a deep 3-quart pot. When melted add the onion and sauté until golden (5 minutes). Add the coarsely grated cabbage, the apple, jelly, salt and red wine. Cover and cook over low heat until tender. *Do not overcook.* Remove from the fire and sprinkle the flour over the cabbage and add the salt. Return pot to the fire and cook until it thickens a bit. Cover and keep hot until ready to serve.

makes 8 servings—freezes well

Note: may be prepared with white cabbage, too.

Baked Celery and Cheese

1 large bunch Pascal celery	2 tbsp butter
2 cups chicken stock	2 tbsp flour
1 small onion	1 cup chopped cooked ham
6 whole cloves	½ cup New England white
⅛ tsp salt	Cheddar cheese, grated
⅛ tsp pepper	

Clean and separate celery. Cut the stalks in approximately 4-inch pieces. Put the chicken stock in a 3-quart pan. Season with the onion, cloves, salt and pepper and add the celery. Cook for 10 minutes or until tender but not mushy. Remove pieces from the pan and set aside until the sauce is prepared. Discard the onion and spices and save the stock for the sauce.

Sauce: Place the butter in a 1-quart pan and when melted remove from heat and add the flour, stirring to keep it smooth. Pour in the remaining stock and mix well to incorporate.

Have ready a flat 1-quart baking dish. Butter it well and lay half of the celery on the bottom. Sprinkle on the ham and on top of ham add some of the grated cheese. Add more celery, ham and cheese. Bake in a preheated 400° oven for 20 minutes. Serve directly from the dish.

makes 4 servings

Braised Celery

1 bunch Pascal celery	⅛ tsp salt
1 tbsp butter	⅛ tsp pepper
1 small onion, minced	1 tsp butter
1 cup chicken or beef stock	

Wash and scrub the celery, then cut the stems into 2-inch pieces. Melt the butter in an 8-inch skillet. Add the onion and cook until golden (approximately 5 minutes). Add the pieces of celery, then the stock, salt and pepper to taste. Cover and cook until the celery is tender (approximately 15-20 minutes). The stock should be absorbed, but if any remains, drain it. Add the teaspoon of butter to make the celery shine and place in a deep serving dish.

makes 4 servings

Boston Baked Beans

2 cups dried navy beans
1½ quarts water
¼ lb salt pork
½ tsp salt
¼ cup dark brown sugar
1 tsp mustard seed
2 tbsp chopped onions
½ cup dark molasses

Wash the beans, then boil in water for 2 minutes. Set aside and soak them in the same water overnight. When ready to cook, add the salt pork and salt and simmer for 1½ hours or until beans are tender. Drain off all but ½ cup of liquid. Place the beans in a 3-quart casserole. Combine the liquid, sugar, mustard seed, onions and molasses and pour mixture over the beans. Bake uncovered in a preheated (10 minutes) 350° oven for 1 hour or until top is browned. Serve from the same casserole.

makes 8 servings

Lima Bean Bake

3 tbsp butter
¼ cup chopped onions
1½ cups tomatoes (cooked
    or canned)
⅛ tsp salt
⅛ tsp pepper
1 tsp sugar
2 cups lima beans
    (fresh or frozen)
¼ cup dried bread crumbs
3 tbsp grated Cheddar cheese

Heat butter in a 1-quart pan. Sauté the onion until it is golden. Add the tomatoes, salt and pepper to taste, the sugar and lima beans (if fresh, cook 7 minutes until tender before adding). Stir well and pour into a 1-quart casserole. Sprinkle the top with the bread crumbs and the cheese. Bake in a 400° oven for 15 minutes or until the cheese is melted and the crumbs are golden brown on top.

makes 6 servings

Spinach Timbale

2 tbsp butter	1 cup milk
1 small onion, chopped	½ cup dried bread crumbs
1 pkg frozen leaf spinach	⅛ tsp salt
or 1 lb fresh spinach,	⅛ tsp pepper
cleaned	⅛ tsp nutmeg
5 whole eggs	

Melt 1 tablespoon of the butter in a small pan. Cook the onion until golden (5 minutes). Add the spinach, cover and cook 5 minutes or until spinach is wilted. Do not drain. Place the eggs, milk, crumbs and seasonings in a large bowl and stir until they are blended. Add the spinach mixture and stir till all ingredients are incorporated, then pour into a greased 1-quart casserole. Bake 1 hour in a preheated 350° oven. Remove from the oven and cover with 1 cup of white sauce if desired.

makes 8 servings

Baked Acorn Squash

2 tbsp butter
3 acorn squash
3 tbsp dark brown sugar
⅛ tsp salt
⅛ tsp pepper
⅛ tsp ground cinnamon

Wash each squash and cut it in half. Slice off a bit of the bottom of each squash half so it will lie flat. Remove pits with a spoon. Divide the butter into six pieces and put a piece into each half. Sprinkle each half with the sugar, salt, pepper and cinnamon. Place the halves in a baking dish and bake in a preheated 400° oven for 30 minutes. Maple syrup or honey may be substituted for the sugar.

makes 6 servings

Baked Winter Squash

        1 lb winter squash
        2 tbsp butter
        ⅛ tsp salt
        ¼ cup dark brown sugar, maple
            syrup or honey
        ⅛ tsp pepper

Wash squash, cut open and remove the seeds and the outer peel. Cut into squares and place in a buttered baking dish. Sprinkle your choice of sweetening over the squash and place the dish in a preheated 400° oven for 45-60 minutes or until the squash is tender. If it dries out, add some chicken stock or water (¼ cup) and continue to bake uncovered until it is done to your taste. Add the salt and pepper in the last 15 minutes of baking.

makes 4 servings

Northern Succotash

2 slices bacon	1/8 tsp salt
1 lb fresh lima beans	1/8 tsp pepper
6 ears fresh corn	1/8 tsp nutmeg
1 fresh tomato	

Cut the bacon in very small pieces and place in a 1-quart pot. Cook on low heat until the fat is rendered from the bacon. Pour off some of the fat. Shell the lima beans and cut the corn from the cob. Peel the fresh tomato by inserting a fork at the stem end and twirling it over an open flame.. This will "pop" the skin and it will be very easy to remove. Cut the tomato in half, then each half in thin slices. Add the lima beans, corn and the tomato to the pot, cover and cook over very low heat for 10 minutes until all vegetables are tender, but not overcooked. Season with salt, pepper and nutmeg. Pour into a deep serving dish and serve.

makes 6 servings

Southern Succotash

1 lb small green beans
6 ears fresh corn
2 tbsp butter
⅛ tsp salt
⅛ tsp pepper

Wash and cut the beans. Cut the corn from the cob. Place butter in a 1-quart pot, add the beans and corn, cover and cook over very low heat for 10 minutes until tender. Do not overcook.

makes 6 servings

Green Beans á la Vinaigrette

2 tbsp olive oil
1 large clove garlic, crushed
1 lb green beans or 1
  pkg frozen beans

⅛ tsp salt
⅛ tsp pepper
1 tbsp vinegar
⅛ tsp sugar

Heat the oil in a small pan, add the garlic and cook until the garlic is golden. Add the beans and salt and pepper and cook until the beans are tender. Before removing, add the vinegar and sugar and toss until all the beans are covered. Place in an attractive bowl and store in the refrigerator until ready to serve.

makes 8 servings

Burgundy Onions

4 very large onions
¾ cup red wine,
    preferably Burgundy
1 tablespoon honey
⅛ tsp salt
⅛ tsp pepper

Slice onions very thin and set aside. Pour the Burgundy or other red wine into a 10-inch skillet. Add the onions, honey, salt and pepper. Cover and cook until they are tender and have taken on the color of the wine. One tablespoon of butter may be added just before serving to give the onions a shine. Serve hot or cold.

makes 6-8 servings

Baked Onions

6 medium onions
1 tbsp olive oil
⅛ tsp salt
⅛ tsp white pepper
1 cup cream sherry

Cut the onions in half and place them cut-side-up in a shallow baking dish. Sprinkle the tops with the olive oil, salt and pepper. Add the wine and bake in a preheated 350° oven for 30 minutes or until the tops of the onions are caramelized and the onions tender. Basting the onions with the wine will help to caramelize them. Serve hot or cold, as a first course or as a vegetable.

makes 4 servings

Candied Sweet Potatoes

6 medium-size sweet potatoes
3 tbsp melted butter
½ cup dark brown sugar
¼ cup rum

Cook sweet potatoes with their jackets in very little water, covered, for 15 minutes or till tender. Remove, cool and set aside until ready to use. To bake: Peel the sweet potatoes and cut lengthwise into ¼-inch slices. Place half of the butter on bottom of a 9 x 6 x 2 dish, reserving half for the top. Sprinkle half of the dark brown sugar over the butter. Place the slices side-by-side, sprinkle with the remaining butter and sugar, and when dish is filled pour the rum over it. Bake in preheated 350° oven for 25 minutes so top is brown and glazed.

makes 8 servings

Baked Apple and Sweet Potato Casserole

6 sweet potatoes	¼ cup dark brown sugar
3 apples	⅛ tsp cinnamon
2 tbsp melted butter	⅛ tsp allspice
½ cup orange juice	¼ cup rum

Boil or steam the potatoes until tender. Remove the skin and cut lengthwise into slices. Peel and core the apples and slice in rings. Grease (with butter) a 9 x 6 x 2 baking dish and alternate layers of potato and apple slices until the dish is filled. Pour over it the orange juice, sugar, seasonings, rum and the other tablespoon of butter. Bake in a preheated 350° oven for 30 minutes. The top should be lightly brown and shiny and the liquid should be absorbed.

makes 6 servings

Sweet Potato and Cranberry Casserole

5 sweet potatoes, cooked
& cooled
Grated rind of 1 orange
½ cup orange juice
¼ cup dark brown sugar
⅛ tsp salt
1 cup whole cranberries, cooked
(fresh or canned)

Grease a 10 x 6 x 2 shallow baking dish with butter. Cut potatoes in half lengthwise and arrange on the bottom of the dish. Combine the orange rind, juice and sugar with the salt and pour over the potatoes. Pour the cranberries over the potatoes. Place in a preheated 375° oven and bake for 25-30 minutes.

makes 8 servings—freezes well

Baked Vegetable Garden

2 tbsp butter
1 lb fresh spinach or 1 pkg
   (10 oz) frozen
2 green peppers, chopped
1 medium onion, chopped
1 large fresh tomato, chopped
⅛ tsp salt
¼ tsp chili powder
⅛ tsp allspice
½ cup dried bread crumbs
½ cup mild Cheddar cheese,
   coarsely grated

Grease a 1-quart casserole with 1 tablespoon of butter and have ready to receive the vegetables. If spinach is fresh, wash it well, dry and toss over heat in the remaining tablespoon of melted butter until tender (3 minutes). If frozen, place in an 8-inch pan with cover and cook 5 minutes till tender. Combine with the peppers, onion and tomato. Add the seasonings and the bread crumbs and pour into the casserole. Mix the cheese and additional bread crumbs and sprinkle over the top. Bake in a preheated 400° oven for 35-40 minutes or until vegetables are just tender, not soft.

makes 8 servings

Farmer's Cabbage Salad

1 medium head cabbage
  (2 cups, shredded)
1 cucumber
1 green pepper

1 cup sliced radishes
2 tbsp minced onion
2 medium tomatoes,
  diced

Coarsely shred the cabbage into a large bowl. Dice the cucumber and green pepper and add. Then add the sliced radishes, the onion and lastly the tomatoes. Mix well and pour over it the following dressing:

½ cup sour cream
1 tbsp honey
⅛ tsp salt

2 tbsp lemon juice or
  vinegar
⅛ tsp paprika

Mix the dressing with a wire whisk in a small bowl and pour over the vegetables. Mix well and serve.

makes 6 servings

Cranberry Coleslaw

1 medium head cabbage (2 cups,
   shredded)
¼ cup fresh cranberries
1 tbsp honey
¼ cup mayonnaise
1 tbsp vinegar

Shred a medium head of cabbage and place in a large bowl. Crush berries with fork or wire whisk. Place the cranberries, honey, mayonnaise and vinegar in a small bowl and beat with a whisk to incorporate the dressing. Pour this over the cabbage and toss lightly to cover.

makes approximately 2½ cups or 6 servings

Fresh Mushroom Salad

1 lb fresh white mushrooms
3 tbsp lemon juice
(1 lemon)
3 tbsp honey
3 tbsp salad oil
Chopped fresh parsley
Chopped fresh chives

"Wash" the mushrooms by dipping a paper towel under water and wiping each mushroom carefully. Remove the stems and save for another dish. Slice the mushrooms thin and place in a bowl. Combine the lemon juice, honey and salad oil; beat with a wire whisk or fork and pour over the mushrooms. Before serving, sprinkle on the fresh parsley and chives.

makes 6 servings

ALL KINDS OF BREADS

Certain days were set aside for the chore of baking, and the baked goods, enough for a week or a fortnight, were kept in cellars to preserve freshness. The baking oven, which was built into one side of the regular fireplace, usually had an iron door that kept out the odors of the food cooking below and sealed in the heat. Long-handled spatulas were fashioned to remove the baked goods from these ovens, as they were deep enough to hold a quantity of food at once.

Colonial women baked all kinds of breads, biscuits and buns, and they modified their recipes to fit the ground wheat, rye, oats and corn that were kept in special rooms to ripen. The milk, cream, butter and eggs needed for baking were produced by the family cow and chickens. Their yeast and baking soda were homemade.

One must remember that the breads the women prepared had little resemblance to what we eat today. These were breads that were made from whole-grain flours which they obtained by crushing the grain between two huge stones. The flour contained all but the coarsest part of the outer covering, the whole of the starch and the germ present in the grain. These breads were not only hearty but wholesome, and they played a big part in maintaining the strength of the colonists.

Oatmeal Bread

1 cup oats	¼ cup lukewarm water
2 tbsp butter	½ cup corn syrup
1¾ cups boiling water	4-5 cups all-purpose flour
2 pkg dry yeast	Butter for greasing pans

Place the oats and butter in a 5-quart bowl. Pour the boiling water over them and let cool. Heat ¼ cup water to lukewarm in a small pan and sprinkle over it the dry yeast. Let stand until bubbly. Stir this into the oat mixture. Add the corn syrup and enough flour to make a stiff dough. Turn out the dough on a floured working area and knead until the dough is smooth and elastic (approximately 5 minutes). Place the dough in a greased bowl and let it rise until it is double in bulk (approximately 1 hour). Punch down and divide the dough into 3 pieces. Roll each piece to form an oval. Place each loaf in a greased 5 x 3 x 1½ bread pan and let rise until it reaches the top of the pan. Bake in a preheated 375° oven for 25 minutes. You may also make this dough into one large loaf; in this case bake it for 50 minutes.

makes 3 small loaves or 1 very large loaf

Sweet Potato Bread

¼ cup butter

¼ cup dark brown sugar

2 whole eggs

1¼ cups mashed cooked
   sweet potatoes

2 tbsp milk

1 tsp lemon juice

2 cups flour

4 tsp baking powder

½ tsp salt

1 cup chopped nuts

¼ cup orange marmalade

Butter for greasing pans

Place the butter with the sugar in a 5-quart bowl and cream until smooth. Add the eggs, potatoes, milk, lemon juice and marmalade and mix well. Then add flour, nuts and lastly the baking powder. Butter three 5 x 3 x 2 small bread pans, divide the batter evenly among them and spread the marmalade on top. Bake in a preheated 350° oven for 30-35 minutes, then remove to a cake rack.

makes 3 small or 1 large loaf—freezes well

Note: Can be baked in a 9 x 5 x 3 pan, but baking time would be 55-60 minutes.

Whole Wheat Bread

1 cup lukewarm water
¼ tsp sugar
3 pkg dry yeast
1 cup whole milk
1 cup molasses
4 cups whole wheat flour

2 cups all-purpose flour
3 tbsp melted butter
1 tsp salt
¼ cup dark brown sugar
Butter for greasing bowl

Heat water in a small pan to lukewarm and pour into a measuring cup. Add sugar and sprinkle on the yeast. Let bubble (5 minutes). Heat the milk and molasses in a small pan until milk is scalded. Cool and pour into a 5-quart bowl. Add the two kinds of flour, butter, salt and the dark brown sugar. Pour in cooled yeast mixture and with a wooden spatula mix until all is incorporated. Turn dough out on a floured working area and knead 1 minute. Place back in same bowl greased with an additional tablespoon of butter and let rise until double (approximately 1½ hours). When double, turn out again on floured working area and divide the dough into 4 pieces. Knead each piece and form into an oval loaf. Place the loaves on large cookie tin and let rise again until double. Brush top with egg wash. Bake in preheated 400° oven for 25-30 minutes.

Egg wash: 1 egg yolk + 1 tablespoon water mixed together

makes 4 small loaves—freezes well

Quick Rye Bread

½ cup lukewarm water ¼ cup dark brown sugar
2 pkg dry yeast   1 whole egg
2 cups rye flour   1 tsp salt
1 cup milk   2 tbsp caraway seeds
¼ cup butter   2 cups all-purpose flour

Heat the water to lukewarm in a small cup and sprinkle on the yeast. Let proof until bubbly (5 minutes). Place the rye flour in a 5-quart bowl. Put the milk, butter and sugar in a 1-quart pan and heat until the milk is scalded. Pour this into the bowl and let cool a bit. Add the egg, salt, caraway seeds and the all-purpose flour, mixing well with a wooden spatula to be sure all ingredients are incorporated. Turn the dough out on a working area dusted with flour and knead for 2-3 minutes to smooth the dough. Put 1 table-spoon of melted butter in the bowl and return the dough to the bowl, turning in the butter to cover and prevent dryness. Let rise until double, then turn out again and divide into three parts, rolling each part into a small loaf and placing it on a cookie tin. Brush tops with egg wash and sprinkle on some more caraway seeds. Let rise again and bake in a preheated 375° oven for 25 minutes.

Egg wash: 1 egg yolk + 1 tablespoon water mixed together

makes 3 small loaves—freezes well

Bran Bread

1 pkg dry yeast
⅓ cup lukewarm water
1 cup whole bran
½ cup water
1 stick butter (¼ lb)
1 whole egg
3 cups flour

Place water in a small bowl and sprinkle on yeast. Let bubble (approximately 5 minutes). Mix the bran and water in a 1-quart pan and let come to a boil, then transfer to a large bowl and let cool until lukewarm. Add the butter, egg and flour and mix well to incorporate all the ingredients. Turn out on a floured working area and knead for 2-3 minutes or until the dough is smooth. Place in a greased bowl, cover and put in the refrigerator until ready to bake. To bake, turn out, punch down again and divide in half. Roll each half into a loaf and place in greased 5 x 3 x 1½ bread pans. Let rise again until dough comes to top of pan. Bake in a preheated 375° oven for approximately 25 minutes.

makes 2 small loaves

Three-Meal Bread

3 cups water	1 whole egg
½ cup sugar syrup	1 cup cornmeal
2 pkg yeast	2 cups whole wheat flour
3 tbsp melted butter	5 cups all-purpose flour
1 tsp salt	

Heat 1 cup of the water to lukewarm. Add 1 tablespoon of the sugar syrup to it, then sprinkle the yeast over it. Set aside to proof. In a 5-quart bowl, add the rest of the sugar syrup, the butter, salt, egg and the flours and mix with a heavy wooden spoon until well blended. Add the rest of the water, mix again and turn out on a working area dusted with all-purpose flour. Knead a minute or two until dough is smooth. Heat 1 tablespoon butter in a small pan, pour it into the empty bowl and return the dough, turning it so that the buttered side is on top. This keeps the dough from drying. Let rise until double (approximately 1 hour), then turn out again onto a floured working area. Cut the dough in thirds and place each piece in a greased loaf pan. Let rise again until it reaches the top of the pan. Brush with egg wash. Bake in preheated 375° oven for 25-30 minutes. Test for doneness with cake tester.

Egg wash: 1 egg yolk + 1 tablespoon water mixed together

makes 3 loaves—freezes well

Beer Bread

1 cup beer	2 cups all-purpose flour
1 pkg dry yeast	1 cup whole wheat flour
3 tbsp melted butter	½ tsp salt
½ cup dark brown sugar	Butter for greasing pan

Heat the beer to lukewarm in a 1-quart pan. Remove from heat and sprinkle on the yeast. Add a pinch of the sugar to start fermentation and set the pan aside until the mixture bubbles (approximately 5 minutes). Place 2 tablespoons of the butter, the sugar, flours and salt in a 5-quart bowl. Mix well to incorporate, then add the yeast mixture and mix again. Turn the batter out on a floured working area and knead a minute or two or until smooth. Grease the bowl with the remaining tablespoon of butter, return the dough to the bowl and turn to coat with butter. Let rise until double in bulk (approximately 1 hour). Turn out again on the working area, knead another minute. Shape into a loaf and place in a greased 9 x 5 x 3 bread pan. Brush the top with butter and let rise until the dough reaches the top of the pan. Bake in a preheated 375° oven for 1 hour.

makes 1 loaf—freezes well

Raisin Casserole Bread

½ stick butter (⅛ lb)   1 cup lukewarm water
1 cup milk   2 pkg yeast
½ cup granulated sugar   1 whole egg
1 tbsp caraway seeds   4½ cups flour
½ tsp salt   1 cup seedless raisins

Place the butter and milk in a 1-quart pan and heat until milk is scalded and butter melted. While hot, add the sugar, caraway seeds and salt. Heat the water to lukewarm, add ¼ teaspoon of sugar to start fermentation and add the yeast. Let stand until bubbly (approximately 5 minutes). Pour this mixture into a 5-quart bowl and add the milk mixture to this. Add the egg and the flour and mix with a wooden spoon to make a firm batter. Let the dough rise in the bowl until double in volume. When double, stir the batter down with the wooden spoon and add the raisins. Turn out on a floured working area and knead the dough about 2 minutes to smooth it. Cut the dough in half and place each half in a greased 1-quart casserole. Let rise until double in bulk (approximately 1 hour). Bake in a preheated 350° oven for 40 minutes. For a shiny top brush with melted butter before baking.

makes 2 loaves—freezes well

Squash Bread with Rum and Liqueur

1½ cups cooked squash

4 whole eggs

1 cup dark brown sugar

¾ cup peanut oil

4 cups all-purpose flour

¼ cup rum

¼ cup orange liqueur

½ tsp nutmeg

½ tsp cinnamon

1 cup chopped nuts

4 tsp baking powder

In the bowl of the electric mixer, place the squash, the eggs, sugar, oil, flour, rum, liqueur and seasonings and mix until well blended. Add nuts (optional) and add the baking powder last, stirring to incorporate. Butter 4 small 7 x 4 x 2 pans and divide the batter between them. Bake in a preheated 350° oven for 40-45 minutes.

makes 4 small loaves

Oven Cornbread

1 cup all-purpose flour

1 cup yellow cornmeal

½ tsp salt

¼ cup sugar

¾ cup milk

1 whole egg

¼ cup melted butter

4 tsp baking powder

In a 5-quart bowl, combine the flour, cornmeal, salt and sugar. Add the milk, the egg and the melted butter. Add the baking powder last. Mix well and pour into greased corn stick molds or into a 9 x 9 x 2¼ pan. Bake in a preheated 400° oven for 20 minutes. Batter must be on the thin side.

makes 14 corn sticks or 1 square loaf—freezes well

Walnut Honey Bread

1 cup milk
½ stick butter (¼ cup)
1 cup honey
¼ cup dark brown sugar
⅛ tsp salt
2 whole eggs
2 cups all-purpose flour
½ cup chopped walnuts
1 tsp baking soda
1 tbsp butter for greasing pans

Scald milk and melt butter in a 3-quart pan. Remove from fire, add honey and sugar. Stir until they are dissolved. Let mixture cool and add the salt, eggs one at a time, the flour and walnuts. Add the baking soda last. Grease two small 7 x 5 x 3 pans with the tablespoon of butter. Pour in the batter, dividing it between the pans. Bake in a preheated 350° oven for 35 minutes or until top is browned. Test for doneness with a cake tester. Remove from oven, place on cake rack and let cool.

makes 2 small loaves—freezes well

Hot Cross Buns

½ cup lukewarm water	½ cup granulated sugar
2 pkg yeast	2 whole eggs
½ cup milk	3-3½ cups all-purpose flour
¼ cup butter	1 cup currants
⅛ tsp salt	1 tsp ground cardamon seed

Heat water to lukewarm in a 1-cup measuring cup, then sprinkle on the yeast. Mix and set aside to bubble (approximately 5 minutes). Heat the milk in a 1-quart pan with the butter just to the boiling point, then remove the pan and ·add the salt and sugar and pour into a 5-quart bowl to cool. When cool, add the eggs one at a time, mixing well, then the flour, currants and cardamon. Turn out on a floured working area and knead for 2-3 minutes to smooth the dough. Melt 1 tablespoon of butter and pour it into the same bowl. Take dough and roll it around in the butter so the top of the dough is greased to prevent drying out. Let it rest in the bowl until it is double in bulk. When double, remove dough, cut in half and roll each half into a rectangle approximately 10 inches long and 12 inches wide. Roll up each rectangle tightly and cut each roll into 12 pieces. Form each piece into a round bun and place side by side in a greased 9 x 9 x 2¼ pan. Let rise again. Do the same with the other half of the dough. Bake in a preheated 375° oven for 20 minutes or until top is lightly brown. Remove from oven to cake rack and ice each bun with a cross piped out on top. Icing: ½ cup confectioners' sugar + ¼ cup water.

makes 24 buns—freezes well

Blueberry Muffins

1 cup blueberries
2 cups all-purpose flour
¼ cup melted butter
½ cup granulated sugar
1 whole egg
1 cup milk
⅛ tsp salt
3 tsp baking powder
Butter for greasing muffin tin

Wash berries and dry well. Mix them with ¼ cup of the flour and set aside. Place sifted flour in a 5-quart bowl, add the butter, sugar, eggs, milk, salt and berries. Add the baking powder last. Fill 12 greased muffin tins ¾ full with batter and bake in preheated 400° oven for 25-30 minutes.

makes 12 muffins—freezes well

Gingerbread

½ cup butter
½ cup sugar
1 whole egg
2½ cups all-purpose flour
1½ tsp baking soda
⅛ tsp salt

1 cup dark molasses
¾ cup hot water
¼ cup rum
¼ tsp ground cinnamon
1 tsp ground ginger
½ tsp ground cloves.

Preheat oven to 350°. Place butter in large bowl, add the sugar, then the egg and beat well. Sift flour with soda and salt and add to first mixture alternately with the molasses, water and rum. Add spices and mix well. Pour batter into a greased 9 x 12 x 2 pan and bake for 45 minutes. Remove pan from oven, cool and serve in large squares topped with dabs of whipped heavy cream.

makes 8-10 servings

Whole Wheat-Rum Muffins

1 cup whole wheat flour
1 cup all-purpose flour
⅛ tsp salt
½ cup milk
¼ cup peanut oil or butter
½ cup orange juice

Grated rind of orange
2 tbsp orange marmalade
1 whole egg
3 tbsp rum
3 tsp baking powder

Grease a muffin tin with oil or butter. Place the flours in a large mixing bowl. Add salt, milk, oil or butter (melted), orange juice and rind, marmalade, egg, rum and lastly the baking powder. Mix well to incorporate ingredients. Using a tablespoon, divide the batter between the 12 indentations. Bake 20-25 minutes in a preheated 400° oven.

makes 12 muffins

Tea Scones

3½ cups flour
½ cup sugar
⅛ tsp salt
¾ cup butter
3 whole eggs
¾ cup milk
1 tsp baking powder

Place the flour, sugar and salt in a large bowl. Add the butter and use a pastry blender to incorporate. Add the eggs, milk and the baking powder. Mix well. Place dough on floured working area, flatten to 1-inch thickness and with a 2-inch biscuit cutter cut into rounds. Place on a greased cookie tin and bake in a preheated 425° oven for 12-15 minutes or until lightly brown on top. Serve warm with butter and marmalade.

makes approximately 16 scones

The early colonists were lovers of all kinds of "sweets" and they set elaborate "sweet tables." These might include all kinds of pies, cakes, puddings, many homemade preserves and sauces, as well as pound and fruit cakes. The punches they served were accompanied by small cakes and cookies. No meal ended without sweets. These sweets gave the energy and body warmth needed to carry out heavy chores.

Recipes for many of these desserts were brought to the New World and kept as family treasures. Others originated here, and were notable for combinations of new foods and exotic flavorings.

The familiar fruits from the orchards and an endless variety of berries were the base of many desserts. In addition, sweet potatoes were used in puddings and pies. Cornmeal, combined with eggs, maple sugar, molasses, rum and brandy, was often served in bowls as a sweet.

Molasses and sugar loaves and many spices such as cinnamon, ginger and nutmeg were stored in colonial larders and used to flavor desserts. Colonial wives often added brandy, sherry, rum or bourbon to their sweets for their "keeping quality."

Bread Pudding Supreme with Wine

2 tbsp butter

3 cups milk

2 whole eggs

2 eggs, separated

¼ cup sugar

2 cups diced bread cubes

¼ cup cream sherry

4 tbsp apple jelly or
   orange marmalade

Melt butter in a 3-quart pot. Add the milk and heat until very warm (not boiling). In a very large bowl, place 2 whole eggs and the 2 egg yolks. Beat until light in color (2 minutes) and stir in 2 tablespoons sugar. Set aside the remaining 2 egg whites. Add the bread cubes to the egg mixture, then add the heated milk and lastly the sherry. Mix to incorporate and pour into a greased 1-quart baking dish or soufflé dish. Bake in a preheated 375° oven for 30 minutes. While pudding is baking, beat the remaining egg whites with remaining 2 tablespoons of sugar until stiff. When pudding is baked, remove, spread top with the jelly, then add meringue and return to oven for 2 minutes to brown.

makes 6-8 servings

Plum Pudding with Hard Sauce

3 cups dry bread crumbs
½ cup tart apples, chopped
¾ cup milk
¾ cup dark brown sugar
6 whole eggs
6 tbsp ground suet
    or 6 tbsp butter
½ tsp ground cinnamon

½ tsp ground nutmeg
½ tsp ground cloves
⅛ tsp salt
1 1-lb jar assorted
    candied fruits
1 cup seedless raisins
1 cup currants
½ cup brandy or rum

Place the crumbs in a very large bowl. Add the apples, milk, sugar, eggs, suet or butter, the spices, then the candied fruits, raisins, currants and ¼ cup of the brandy or rum. Use your fingers to work in the fruits. Grease a 2-quart mold with a tablespoon of butter and pack in the mixture. Seal the top securely with either a lid or aluminum foil. If foil, tie with a strong string. Place mold on a rack in the bottom of a large soup pot. Pour enough water into the pot to come halfway up the mold. Cover the pot and steam over medium heat for 4 hours. If necessary add more water to keep the level always the same. When steamed, invert on a deep platter and flambé (flame). To flame: Put the remaining ½ cup of brandy or rum in a ladle and place this close to the flame of the stove. This will ignite in a second. Quickly pour the flaming liquid over the pudding and rush it to the table.

Hard Sauce:
1½ cups confectioners' sugar
½ cup unsalted butter,
    softened
1 egg yolk
3 tbsp brandy or rum

Place sugar and butter in a small bowl and smooth and blend the ingredients with a wooden spatula. Add the egg yolk and then the spirits and stir until you have a very smooth sauce.

makes 8 servings

Indian Pudding

2 cups milk	¼ tsp ground ginger
¼ cup yellow cornmeal	¼ tsp ground nutmeg
2 tbsp butter	¼ tsp allspice
¼ cup molasses	¼ tsp cinnamon
2 whole eggs	⅛ tsp salt

Heat the milk in a double boiler and pour in the cornmeal. Cook for 20 minutes, remove from heat and add the rest of the ingredients. Grease a 1-quart baking dish with butter, pour in the mixture and bake in a preheated 400° oven for 30 minutes. Serve from the same dish.

makes 6 servings

New England Berry Grunt

2 cups berries, any kind	2 tbsp butter
1 cup water	½ cup milk
½ cup sugar	⅛ tsp salt
1½ cups all-purpose flour	3 tsp baking powder

If berries are fresh, wash them well and place them in the water. Add the sugar and cook over low heat until tender but not soft (approximately 5 minutes). Set aside. If berries are frozen, just defrost and set aside; no sugar is needed. For dough: Mix butter into the flour with a pastry blender. Add the milk, salt and baking powder. Have ready a 1-quart heat-proof mold. Grease it well with more butter and pour in the berries. Cover with the dough and over the top lay a piece of aluminum foil. Tie this with a string and immerse the mold in a deep pot. Pour in water to reach halfway up. Cover the pot and simmer for approximately 1½ hours. When finished steaming, turn out on a deep platter and serve with Brandy Sauce.

Brandy Sauce:
    1 cup fresh or canned berries
    ½ cup sugar
    1 cup water
    ¼ cup fruit liqueur or brandy

The sauce must match the pudding. If it is a Cherry Grunt, combine fresh or canned cherries with sugar and water and boil gently until a bit thick. Add cherry brandy last.

makes 6-8 servings

Note: Desserts made with berries topped with biscuit dough and steamed were called grunts because of the noise they made while cooking.

Apple Betty

¼ cup melted butter
4 cups sliced apples
4 cups coarse, stale bread
   crumbs
¾ cup dark brown sugar
1 tsp ground cinnamon
½ tsp ground cloves

Use 2 tablespoons of the butter to grease a 9 x 13 x 2 baking dish. Peel and core the apples, then slice them—approximately 16 slices to the apple—and set aside. Combine the crumbs with butter, sugar and seasonings. Place a layer of crumbs on the bottom of the baking dish, then a layer of the apples, ending with crumbs on top. Bake in a 400° oven for 45 minutes or until top is brown and apples are cooked. Serve hot or cold with a bowl of whipped cream.

makes 8 servings

Pumpkin Pudding with Rum

2 tbsp butter	3 tbsp orange juice
3 tbsp flour	1/8 tsp salt
3/4 cup milk	1/2 tsp ground nutmeg
4 eggs, separated	1/4 tsp ground cinnamon
1 1/2 cups cooked pumpkin	1 tsp ground ginger
1/2 cup dark brown sugar	1/4 cup rum (light or dark)

Melt butter in a 2-quart pan, remove from fire and add flour. Stir in milk and egg yolks. Cook, stirring constantly until thick. Remove from fire and add pumpkin, sugar, orange juice, salt, spices and rum. When ingredients are well blended, put pan back on fire and reheat for a minute. Remove and add the stiffly beaten egg whites. Pour into a 1-quart soufflé dish or bowl and bake at 375° for 30 minutes. Serve immediately.

makes 6-8 servings

Brandied Apple Cake

1/4 cup butter
1/2 cup dark brown sugar

Grease round, 9-inch layer cake pan with butter, sprinkle with brown sugar and set aside.

Batter:

¼ cup butter	1 tsp vanilla
½ cup sugar	¼ cup brandy
2 whole eggs	2 tsp baking powder
1½ cups flour	

Place the butter in electric mixer bowl and blend in the sugar. Add the eggs one at a time, the flour, vanilla, brandy and baking powder. When thoroughly mixed, set aside.

Topping:

2 large baking apples	½ cup water
½ cup sugar	Juice of 1 lemon

Peel the apples and cut in halves, then quarters, cut each quarter into 4 slices, making a total of 16 slices from each apple. In a 10-inch skillet combine the sugar, water and lemon juice. Bring quickly to the boil and lay the slices of apple in the liquid. Cook for approximately 5 minutes or until the liquid in the pan thickens and apples are *just* tender. Carefully remove slices and arrange them on top of the butter-brown sugar mixture in pan. Pour the batter over the apples, being sure to cover entire surface. Bake in a preheated 350° oven for 35 minutes. Remove from oven and quickly invert on a cake rack.

makes 10 servings

Rum Cake

Cake:

6 eggs, separated, or 3 eggs
   & 3 tbsp water
¾ cup sugar
1 tbsp grated lemon rind

1 cup sifted flour
⅛ tsp salt
1 tsp baking powder

Mix egg yolks and sugar in bowl of electric mixer for 1 minute. Add lemon rind, flour and salt. In another bowl beat egg whites until stiff and combine with yolk mixture. Add baking powder and fold all together. Bake in a 10-inch angel food pan for 45 minutes in a 350° oven, remove and cool.

Syrup:

½ cup sugar
1 12-oz can apricot nectar
1 tbsp lemon juice

¼ cup rum
1 cup heavy cream,
   whipped

Place the sugar and apricot nectar in a 1-quart pan and simmer together for 10 minutes. Add lemon juice and rum and set aside to cool.

When both the cake and syrup are cool, put the cake back into the pan it was baked in and gradually pour the syrup over it and allow to rest. When ready to serve, turn out on a platter and fill the center with the whipped heavy cream.

makes 8-10 servings

Simnel Cake

¼ lb butter
1 cup sugar
4 whole eggs
2 cups flour
1 cup seedless raisins
1 cup currants
1 cup sultanas
(yellow raisins)

¼ tsp each of ground
nutmeg, cinnamon,
cloves and allspice
½ cup mixed glacé fruits
¼ cup brandy
2 tsp baking powder
½ tsp almond extract
Almond paste

Place the butter and sugar in a very large bowl and mix well. Add the eggs one at a time, then one cup of the flour alternately with the brandy. Pour the cup of flour and the fruits into another large bowl and mix well with your hand to incorporate and coat the fruits. Add this to the butter, sugar and egg mixture and continue to mix with a wooden spatula or spoon, as the batter is heavy. Add the baking powder and almond extract. Have ready a 10-inch tube pan, well buttered, and pour the batter into it. Bake in a preheated 350° oven for 1 hour. When baked, remove and spread with a layer of almond paste. Decorate with additional red cherries and green pineapple pieces.

makes 10-12 servings

Note: *Lambert Simnel was pretender to the English throne under Henry VII.*

Lemon Pound Cake

2 cups sifted flour	½ cup peanut or corn oil
1¼ cups granulated sugar	Juice & rind of 1 lemon
⅛ tsp salt	¼ tsp cream of tartar
5 egg yolks	6 egg whites
½ cup water	3 tsp baking powder

Place the flour, sugar, salt, yolks and water in a 5-quart bowl. Add oil, lemon juice and rind. Stir with wooden spoon until ingredients are combined. Add the cream of tartar to the egg whites and beat until very stiff. Gently fold the beaten whites into the yolk mixture. Add the baking powder and pour into a greased 10-inch angel food pan. Bake in preheated 350° oven for 1 hour. When baked, turn out on cake rack and pour over it a lemon glaze.

Lemon Glaze:

> 1 egg yolk
> 2 tbsp butter, melted
> 1½ cups confectioners' sugar
> Juice and rind of 1 lemon

Beat the egg yolk in a small bowl till light in color (2 minutes). Add melted butter and approximately 1½ cups confectioners' sugar. Stir all together. Add the juice and rind of the lemon and

beat until consistency is smooth. Spread on cake
and let glaze drip over the sides.

makes 10 servings

Orange Tipple Cake

¼ cup butter	¼ cup chopped nuts
¼ cup shortening	½ cup orange marmalade
1 cup granulated sugar	¼ cup orange liqueur
2 whole eggs	¼ tsp salt
2 cups all-purpose flour	2 tsp baking powder
¼ cup milk	1 tbsp butter for greasing pan

Place the butter and shortening in electric mixer
bowl. Add the sugar and blend on low speed for
2 minutes. Add the eggs one at a time, the flour
and milk, then the nuts, marmalade, liqueur and
salt. Add the baking powder last. Grease a 1½-
quart fancy baking mold with the butter and pour
in the batter. Bake for 45 minutes in a preheated
350° oven. When baked, remove from the oven
to a cake rack and pour on an orange glaze:

Orange Glaze:

½ cup confectioners' sugar

Grated rind of 1 orange

2 tbsp orange liqueur or juice

Combine all ingredients and pour over cake.

makes 8-10 servings—freezes well

German Beer Cake

1 cup dark molasses	¼ tsp ground cinnamon
¼ cup butter or oil	¼ tsp ground cloves
2 whole eggs	¼ tsp ground nutmeg
1 cup dark beer	½ cup chopped walnuts
2½ cups all-purpose flour	1½ tsp baking soda
1 cup seedless raisins	Sesame seeds
½ tsp ground ginger	

Preheat the oven to 350°. In a large bowl mix the molasses and butter or oil. Add the eggs and beat until well blended. Add the beer alternately with the flour. Add the raisins, seasonings, nuts and lastly the baking soda. Bake in a greased 9 x 13 x 2 baking dish for 45 minutes. Remove from the oven and sprinkle top with sesame seeds.

makes 10 servings

Rum and Butter Wafers

½ lb butter
¼ cup verifine sugar
1 egg yolk
2 cups all-purpose flour
1 tbsp rum
2 tbsp wheat germ

Blend the butter and sugar with an electric mixer. Add the egg yolk, flour, rum and wheat germ, mixing on low speed to incorporate ingredients. Remove dough from bowl to a working area, divide in half and roll each half into a "salami-style" roll, sprinkling with a bit of flour to keep dough from sticking. Wrap each roll in aluminum foil and store in refrigerator until ready to bake.

When ready to bake, preheat oven to 375°, then cut the rolls in slices the thickness of a half-dollar. Place on cookie tin and bake for 12 minutes or until very light brown around edges.

makes approximately 5 dozen

Chocolate Rum Chips

2 squares baking chocolate
¼ lb butter
1 cup dark brown sugar
1 whole egg
¼ cup milk
½ tsp dried orange rind
1¾ cups all-purpose flour
¼ cup rum
1 pkg (6 oz) chocolate bits
1 tsp baking powder

Preheat oven to 375°. Melt chocolate over hot water. Cream butter with sugar until sugar is dissolved. Add egg, milk, orange rind and flour alternately with rum. Add melted chocolate, then chocolate bits. Add baking powder last. Drop by teaspoonfuls on cookie sheet and bake for 15 minutes.

makes approximately 3 dozen cookies

Spicy Pumpkin Pie

Pie Shell:

1½ cups all-purpose flour ⅛ tsp salt
½ cup shortening ½ cup ice water

Place flour in a medium-size bowl. Add the shortening and, with a pastry cutter, quickly incorporate. Add the salt and gradually add the water. Mix lightly with a rubber spatula to form a ball. Turn out on a working area and divide in half. Roll one half into a 9-inch circle and place in a greased 9-inch pie plate.

Caution: This operation should take no more than *2 minutes.* Do not overmix. Recipe makes two 9-inch pie shells. Other half of dough can be made into a shell, baked and frozen.

Filling:

⅓ cup boiling water	¾ cup dark brown sugar
⅛ tsp salt	2 cups canned or freshly
2 tsp cinnamon	cooked pumpkin puree
1 tsp ground ginger	4 whole eggs
½ tsp ground nutmeg	1 cup heavy cream

Combine the spices with the water in a small cup. Pour pumpkin in a large bowl and add the water-spice mixture and the sugar. Add the eggs one at a time. Add the cream and mix well. Pour into a prepared 9-inch pie shell and bake in a preheated 450° oven for 10 minutes, then reduce the heat to 350° and bake for 40 minutes. Insert knife to test for doneness. If it comes out clean, it is done.

makes 6 servings

Apple Pie

Crust:

1½ cups all-purpose flour   ½ cup cold water
½ cup shortening   ⅛ tsp salt

Place flour in medium size bowl, add the short-ening and with a pastry blender or your fingers work the shortening into the flour for 2 minutes— *no more!* Add the water and salt and with a rubber spatula quickly gather dough into a ball. Keep in refrigerator until ready to use.

Filling:

3 lbs tart apples   Cinnamon
¼ cup granulated sugar   2 tbsp butter

When ready to bake, remove ball of dough from refrigerator, cut in half and roll one half into a circle to fit into a 10-inch pie plate. Grease pie plate with butter and set the circle of pie crust in it. Peel the apples and cut in quarters, then cut the quarters into thirds. Place these in the pie plate and sprinkle with cinnamon and sugar to your taste. Add butter in small bits. Roll out the other half of the pie crust dough to fit over the apples. Gather the two edges and crimp them, or use the tines of a fork to seal the edges. Place in a preheated 400° oven and bake the pie for 40 minutes. Remove, dust with confec-tioners' sugar and cool on a cake rack.

makes 8-10 servings

Sherry Pie

Crust:

1½ cups leftover chocolate cake
or cookie crumbs
¼ cup butter, melted

Mix together and press into a greased 9-inch pie plate. Bake for 5 minutes in a 350° oven, remove and cool. Set aside to receive filling.

Filling:

3 eggs, separated	⅛ tsp salt
1 cup milk	½ cup cream sherry
½ cup sugar	1 cup whipped cream
1 tbsp unflavored gelatin	¼ cup chopped pecans

In the top of a double boiler place the egg yolks, ¾ cup milk and sugar and cook until the custard thickens. Soften the gelatin in the remaining ¼ cup of milk and add salt. Add to custard and remove from the fire. Add the sherry, the stiffly beaten egg whites and when cool add the whipped cream. Pour into the prepared pie crust and place in the refrigerator overnight to mellow. Before serving, sprinkle with the chopped pecans.

makes 8 servings

Special Peach Pie

Crust:

1½ cups unbleached,
    all-purpose flour
½ cup shortening

½ cup ice water
⅛ tsp salt

Place flour in bowl, work in shortening, add salt and water quickly. Roll out half of the dough and line a 10-inch pie plate. Bake 20 minutes in a 400° oven, then remove and cool on a cake rack. Reserve the rest of dough for another pie.

Pastry Cream:

2 cups milk
½ cup granulated sugar
4 egg yolks

¼ cup flour
2 tbsp peach brandy

Combine the milk, sugar, egg yolks and flour in a 1-quart pan. Beat with a fork or rotary beater to blend. Place pan over low heat and cook until the mixture thickens. Cool well, then add the brandy.

To combine:

2 lb fresh, ripe peaches
1 cup heavy cream

Peel and slice the peaches and place them in the bottom of the pie shell. Pour the pastry cream over the peaches and top with the heavy cream, whipped. Chill in refrigerator until ready to serve.

makes 8-10 servings

DRINKS

Apples served the colonists in pies and pudding, but even more importantly as cider. Next to water, cider was the most abundant and least costly drink to be had in New England. Almost all drank beer, and rum was used as a cure-all for many ills as well as a daily beverage.

From cider and beer the colonists turned to more potent stimulants. They drank Madeira, Claret (Bordeaux red wine) and Burgundy or their own homemade wines. People in better circumstances drank fruit cordials, elderberry and dandelion wine and applejack. Madeira, Port and sweet wines were always served to the ladies after dinner while the men gathered in another room to talk and drink harder rums and brandies. The colonists in the South imported their rum from Jamaica and were the originators of the famed Mint Julep.

It was Thomas Jefferson, a renowned gourmet and host, who brought from abroad not only Madeira but Claret and Burgundies from France and Rhine wines from Germany. He felt that food and wine were the fruits of a benevolent Creator and should be enjoyed; the glories of haute cuisine had a staunch defender in him.

Benjamin Franklin, too, was no stranger to wines and fine food. He was one of the first travelers to use the inns and taverns that were springing up in the new land, and he rated these early hotels by their beer, wine, toddies and food, returning time and again to certain favorites which knew his likes by then.

Hot Buttered Rum

Sugar

Dark rum

Boiling water

Butter

Nutmeg

For each drink, combine 1 teaspoon sugar, ½ cup boiling water, ½ cup dark rum and 1 tablespoon of butter in a tumbler. Fill with additional boiling water and stir all until combined. Serve hot with grated nutmeg on top.

Blue Blazer

Scotch whiskey

Verifine sugar

Boiling water

Lemon peel

Combine a jigger (1½ ounces) of Scotch whiskey and 1 jigger (1½ ounces) boiling water in a mug. Strike a match to ignite the spirits and while the flame burns pour from one mug to another, transferring the flame to each. Add 1 teaspoonful verifine sugar to sweeten it and add a twist of lemon before serving.

makes 1 serving

Note: These drinks were invented by the colonists to ward off the cold of the long winters.

Hot Whiskey Toddy

1 tbsp sugar   1 jigger (1½ oz) whiskey
4 oz boiling water   Twist of lemon peel

Dissolve the sugar in the boiling water right in the glass. Add the whiskey and lemon peel and sprinkle the top with ground nutmeg.

makes 1 serving

Thomas and Jeremiah

1 tsp sugar   3 eggs, separated
1 tsp ground cloves   2 cups bourbon whiskey
1 tsp ground cinnamon   2 cups hot, strong coffee
¼ cup rum

Place the sugar and spices in a bowl with the egg yolks and beat with a wire whisk until the eggs are thick and light in color. Beat the egg whites stiff and fold them into the yolks. Stir until all is incorporated and place the bowl in the refrigerator to mellow overnight. When ready to serve, place a tablespoon of the mixture in each 4-ounce demitasse cup. Add a jigger (1½ ounces) bourbon and a jigger (1½ ounces) each of hot coffee and rum, then stir.

makes 10-12 servings

Hot Spiced Cider

3 lemons	1½ quarts cold water
3 large oranges	1 cup of sugar
1 tsp ground allspice	1 gallon cider
2 sticks cinnamon	

Squeeze the fruit, reserving the juice, and put only the rinds in a 3-quart pot. Add the spices, cover with the cold water, bring to a boil and *simmer* for one hour. Strain the liquid and add the cup of sugar to it. Add the fruit juices and cider in a large pot and bring to a boil. Serve piping hot.

makes 25-30 servings

Hot Wine Punch

1 cup sugar	18 whole cloves
3 cups boiling water	1 stick cinnamon
½ large lemon & rind	2 bottles of red wine
Freshly ground nutmeg	

Place the sugar, water, lemon, cloves and cinnamon in a 3-quart pot. *Simmer* for 15 minutes. Strain out the flavorings and add the red wine. Heat to just the boiling point again and pour into four-ounce punch glasses. Sprinkle some freshly ground nutmeg on top of each glass.

makes 12 servings

Ruby Port Hot Punch

Juice & rind of 1 orange 3 tbsp sugar
Juice & rind of 1 lemon 2 cinnamon sticks
1 quart boiling water 1 26-oz bottle ruby Port
  Nutmeg, freshly grated

Peel the orange and the lemon and place the rinds in a deep pot with the boiling water and cook over very low heat for approximately 15 minutes. Remove from heat and add the juices, sugar, cinnamon sticks and the wine. Place over *simmering* heat for 15 minutes, watching carefully that it does not boil. Serve hot with freshly grated nutmeg on top.

makes 20 servings

Madeira Mist

1 bottle Madeira wine 2 navel oranges, sliced,
2 tbsp brandy. skin on
¼ cup apricot brandy 1 cup pineapple chunks
1 cup granulated sugar

Place the Madeira, brandy, apricot brandy and the sugar in a large pot. Heat slowly to the boiling point and add the orange slices, then the pineapple chunks. Serve piping hot from a punch bowl to get the fruits easily into punch glasses.

makes 6 four-ounce servings

Wassail Bowl

1 gallon apple cider
24 whole cloves
2 tsp ground allspice
5 sticks cinnamon
2 cups orange juice

Juice & rind of 2 large
lemons
2 cups granulated sugar
3 cups apple brandy

Pour the cider, flavorings, orange juice, lemon juice and rind and the sugar into a 5-quart pot and mix well. Bring slowly to the boil and *simmer* for 15 minutes. Strain out flavorings, add the apple brandy and heat to just the boil. Serve piping hot in four-ounce punch glasses.

makes 40 servings

Spanish Bollan

Slices from 1 grapefruit,
peeled
2 tbsp fresh lemon juice
1 bottle red wine

¼ cup ginger wine
¼ tsp nutmeg
¼ tsp cinnamon
½ cup sugar

Marinate the grapefruit slices in the lemon juice for an hour. Heat the wines and spices in a large pot to the boiling point, but *do not boil!* Place a slice of lemon in each glass and pour in the hot wine.

makes 4 six-ounce servings

Mint Julep

Crushed Ice

Mint leaves

Cognac

Jamaican rum

For each drink, fill a deep tumbler with ice and place 3 fresh mint leaves on top. Pour 4 ounces of Cognac and 4 ounces of rum into the glass. Pour back and forth between two tumblers until chilled and glass is frosted.

Note: No two people could ever agree as to the method of mixing, but, as a rule, Mint Juleps were served in deep cut-glass tumblers. Some wealthy families used silver mugs or goblets.

Pink Lemonade

3 lemons

¾ cup sugar

3 cups cold water

½ bottle maraschino

cherries & juice

Wash lemons, dry and cut into very thin slices. Remove any seeds. Place slices in a bowl and add the sugar. Let rest until sugar is dissolved. Add cold water and cherry juice. Add ice cubes to a large pitcher, mix and pour over more ice into six-ounce glasses. Serve with cherries as garnish. In a newer version ½ cup cherry liqueur is added.

makes 6-8 servings

Ye Old Mansion Eggnog

48 eggs, separated
3½ cups granulated sugar
2 bottles rye whiskey
(fifths)
1·23-oz bottle rum
2 tsp cream of tartar
2 quarts heavy cream
Nutmeg

In a very large bowl beat the egg yolks with the sugar until light in color and very thick. Add the whiskey and rum gradually, beating continuously. Add cream of tartar to the egg whites and whip until very stiff. Fold this into the yolks carefully until all the whites are incorporated. Whip the cream until thick and blend it into the mixture. Serve chilled with nutmeg on top of each punch glass.

makes 50 servings

Benjamin Franklin's Orange Shrub

2 quarts orange juice
2 lbs granulated sugar
1 gallon of rum

One month before the party, dissolve the sugar in the orange juice. Mix in the rum and pour the mixture into a wooden cask. Let stand a month to mellow.

makes 50 four-ounce servings

Roman Punch

1 quart lemon sherbet
1 cup Jamaican rum

Mix the rum into the sherbet and spoon the mixture into stemmed clear four-ounce glasses. Place a slice of lemon or a cherry on top for decoration.

makes 4-6 servings

Fish House Punch

2 cups granulated sugar
1 quart lemon juice
2 bottles Jamaican rum (fifths)
1 bottle brandy (fifth)
1 cup peach brandy

Dissolve the sugar in the lemon juice by mixing well. Transfer to a large punch bowl filled with a block of ice or ice cubes from 4 trays. Add the rum and both brandies. Allow to mellow for a few minutes. Stir to blend flavors well before serving in four-ounce punch glasses.

makes 40 servings

Frosty Sherbet Punch

3 46-oz cans orange &
  grapefruit blend
3 12-oz cans apricot
  nectar
3 bottles champagne
3 quarts pineapple sherbet

Have the juices and champagne chilled. Empty 1 can of each juice and 1 bottle of champagne into punch bowl, add 1 quart of sherbet and spoon the liquid over it to melt it. Serve in punch glasses. When supply runs low, repeat.

makes 2½ gallons of punch or 80 four-ounce servings

Haymakers' Switchel

1 cup brown sugar
1 tsp ground ginger
½ cup molasses
¾ cup vinegar

2 quarts water
1 cup hard cider or
  brandy

Combine all the ingredients and keep refrigerated until ready to serve. Place ice in very large pitcher, add chilled switchel and pour over more ice in six-ounce glasses.

makes 8-10 servings

Index